Spans & Layers

Handbook

Steffen Parratt

Introduction

Without disciplined efforts to stay fit, firms often grow to be bloated, bureaucratic and inefficient. Reducing layers of management and increasing manager spans of control is a time-tested method for improving a firm's fitness.

Let's begin with an example to define a few terms. The tiny company shown below has eleven employees: five are managers and six are independent contributors. *Managers* have direct reports, and *independent contributors* do not.

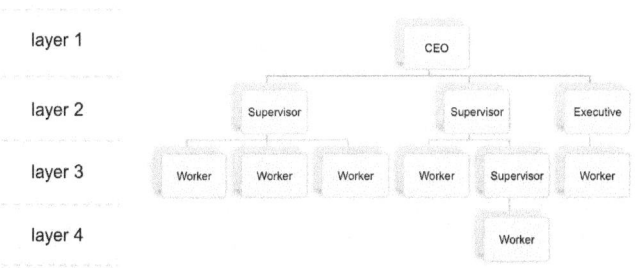

There are four layers in this organization, from the CEO on layer 1, to the Worker on layer 4. *Layers* are defined by reporting relationships. The CEO and one Supervisor have a *span of control* of three (i.e., each has three direct reports). The second Supervisor has a span of control of two. The Executive and the third Supervisor have a span of control of one. Independent contributors (i.e., Workers) do not have a span of control because they lack direct reports.

This organization can benefit from layer and span optimization. *Layer optimization* is a process of reassigning or eliminating managers who create unnecessary layers. Below we have identified a Supervisor overseeing one Worker. This Supervisor is a candidate for optimization because he has a low span of control, as does his manager. Layer optimization would identify him as a candidate for elimination from this part of the organization. Let's assume this Supervisor is redundant and is removed.

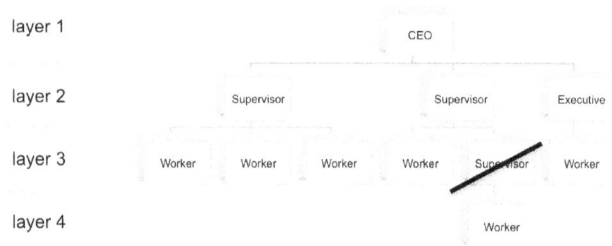

The organization now has three layers.

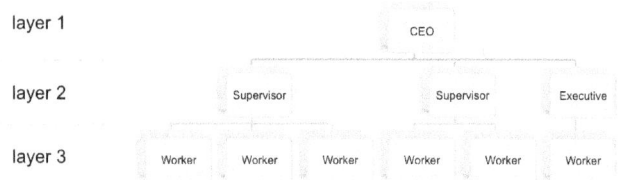

Span of control optimization is the process of re-assigning or eliminating managers with suboptimal spans of control. The CEO and one Supervisor have a span of control of three, the other Supervisor has a span of two, and the Executive as has a span of one.

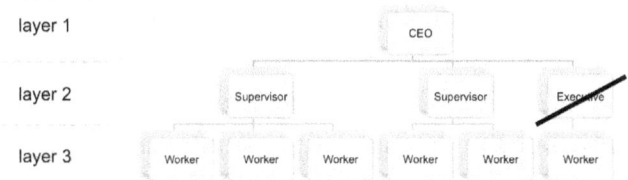

If a typical manager can oversee three direct reports, then there is an opportunity to combine workers under either the Supervisor or the Executive. In this case we have eliminated the Executive, yielding the final optimized organization shown below.

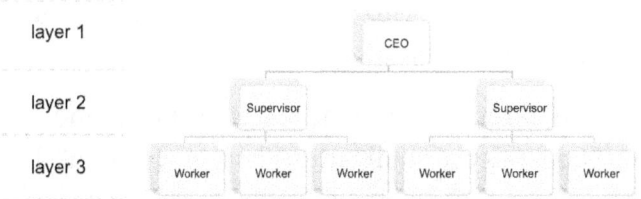

By eliminating two managers, we have reduced management by 40% and have increased the average span of control by a similar degree. Of course, layer and span optimization are easy for this simple example. In reality, for large organizations the process is much more onerous and requires a systematic process and software.

For a given number of employees, a higher average span of control implies a lower number of management layers. The appropriate span of control for a firm depends on several factors, including its industry, the type of work it performs and its geographic reach. There are some established rules of thumb for different types of firms. Also, benchmarking against similar firms may help you understand if your firm has an appropriate span and layer structure.

Organizations that successfully flatten and widen their management hierarchies don't just save money; case studies have shown that these organizations also have improved decision making, enhanced accountability, faster and more reliable communication, are more efficient, and their employees are happier.

If lean, flat organizations are superior, then why do companies' organizations become bloated? The same reason that sedentary humans recognize the benefits of fitness, but grow out of shape; weight gain and body shape changes are slow and insidious. If an organization does not periodically check its fitness, then it too will gradually get out of shape. Often an organization doesn't realize it has too many management layers or a span of control problem until its cost structure becomes out of line with industry benchmarks. After a company works itself into a fit condition, it needs to periodically check its spans and layers to ensure that it remains fit.

Like any person trying to get fit, starting the process can be the hardest part. Furthermore, if the goal of the project is to reduce expenses, then the last thing you want to do is to hire expensive management consultants to solve your problem. This Handbook is designed specifically for firms in this situation.

About this book

This is the *Spans & Layers* volume of our "Single Sitting Simplification Series"

- Single Sitting – leaders are busy and do not have the time to read management tomes. Each volume of the series can be read within a single sitting, maybe over lunch, or on the train ride home.

- Simplification – this is not an exposition of new ideas in the theory of management. Instead, it is an aggregation of principles and practices relevant to organization optimization.

- Series – this one of a series of volumes that addresses the major topics relevant to leading a company.

It is a brief book, to the point, something that you carry around with you, scribbling in the margins, until you have completed the job. We are passionate about simplification; we have authored a simple book.

Opportunity

We all have heard that flatter organizations are superior to organizations with long reporting lines, but why? Simply because deep layers of management lead to several issues:

- Communication is diminished: communication from the leaders to the employees, and from customers to the leaders. It's like the childhood game of "telephone", the more people in the communication chain the more the message becomes changed and garbled.

- Accountability is diminished. If your boss gives you a task, you are accountable. If you are able to delegate that task to an underling, who can delegate to his/her underling, etc, then accountability for the task is diluted or lost completely.

- Efficiency is diminished. Which is more efficient, one 15-person staff meeting or five 3-person staff meetings? Does it make sense to have managers go through the entire HR training, performance evaluation training, etc, each year for a couple of employees? Executives who spend part of their time managing and part of their time as an individual contributor may do neither function well.

- Decision-making is compromised. In an environment with poor communication, poor accountability, and inefficient management processes, decision-making is hampered.

- Wasted effort: unnecessary managers create or continue unnecessary work to justify their existence. Have you ever noticed that when some managers leave, they don't need to be replaced? Resource limitations are a great way to focus on essential activities.

- High expenses: unnecessary managers doing unnecessary work are an expensive drag on the organization. Compensation for your management team will be reduced by the need to pay unnecessary managers.

- Morale suffers: poor communication, lack of accountability, inefficiencies, poor decisions, high expenses, lower compensation and unnecessary managers doing unnecessary work, all lead to poor morale. Unnecessary managers are in constant fear of losing their jobs and spend time and mental energy looking for opportunities outside of the company, poisoning the work environment.

For humans, the benefits of physical fitness are obvious and undeniable. However, fitness requires discipline, some work, and good habits.

The same is true for organizational fitness. Lean organizations, with high spans of control, and fewer layers of management are superior. The next section describes a common redesign process organizations use to increase their management spans of control and reduce layers of management.

Approach

The first step is to determine if your company has a problem. A diagnostic analysis is required to determine your firm's average manager spans of control and the number of layers for the entire firm and for each division, function and region. This is often addressed with software tools.

Let's assume we have evaluated the organization and we find that it is over-managed (i.e., there are too many managers) and there are redundant managers. Fine, but what do you do about it? Can software redesign the organization for us too? Unfortunately not, it requires old-fashioned hard work to restore the organization to fitness. How much work you need to do depends on the extent of the problem. If the problem is contained in one division, function or region, then you can focus on that one area alone. However, if the problem is pervasive, then you will need to consider the entire organization.

Spans and layers optimization is a top-down process. If you are addressing the entire company, then the process begins with the company's CEO. There are several reasons why we start at the top, but the most important is that each manager (with the help of a company's Reengineering Team or consultants) must redesign the layer below him or her. Starting at the top makes a lot of sense. We'll make these concepts more concrete through an example.

For our hypothetical company, the CEO resides on layer 1 and his or her direct reports on layer 2. These two layers are special cases, for several reasons. To begin with, layer 1 has only one employee (the CEO), so redesign possibilities are limited. CEOs generally have high spans of control and therefore there isn't much work to be done on layer 2. Given its importance to the company, layer 2 typically has already been designed carefully and reviewed periodically. The real work usually begins on layer 3.

The figure below shows the organization chart for Business Head 1 on layer 2 and his direct reports on layer 3. Of course we would have to follow the same process for all the other managers on layer 2, but we will focus on a single manager (Business Head 1) for discussion purposes. We have also shown the direct reports on layer 4, although we have excluded their titles for simplicity.

Business Head 1 is responsible for redesigning the layer that reports to him. He needs to have detailed knowledge of the responsibilities of his managers and may have to make some difficult decisions about who stays and who goes. However, he is not responsible for conducting the redesign process itself, which in itself is a full-time job. A company reengineering team, possibly a special task force, or a consulting company, should manage the process.

As you think about who will be in charge of your company's redesign process, there are a few considerations to keep in mind. Ideally you should choose a team that has this process as part of its mandate. That way the team will develop expertise in the process and will be able to run the process periodically, and will not have to reinvent the wheel each time.

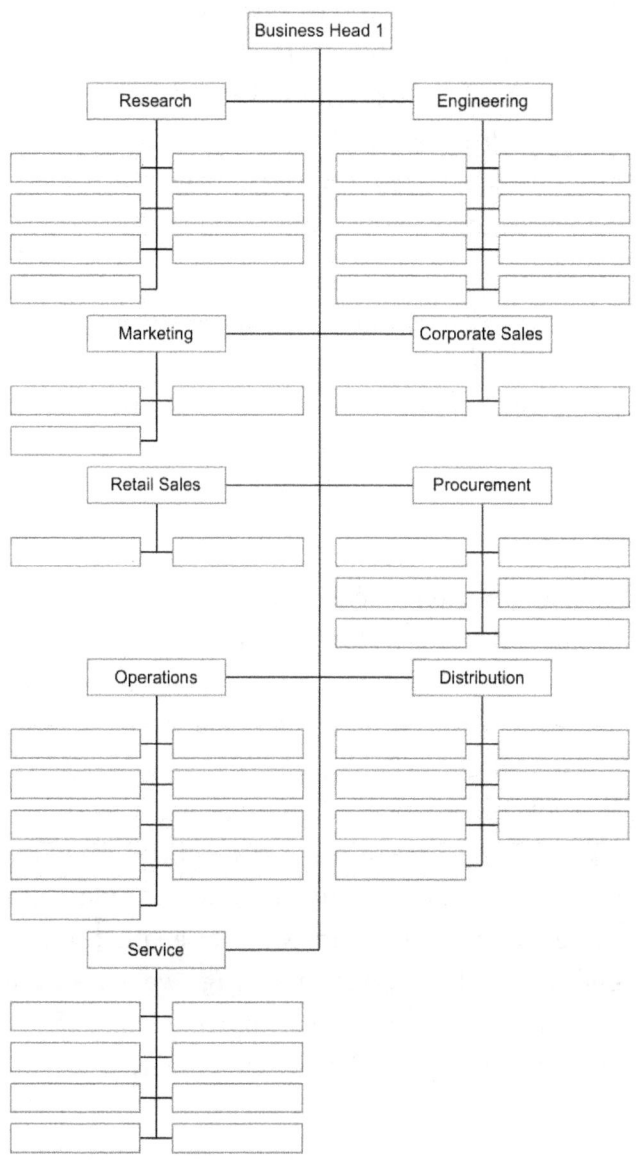

The team running the redesign process (let's assume it is the company's Reengineering Team) will need to guide Business Head 1 in the redesign of his organization, but also look across other groups on layer 3 to see if there are any synergies across the company.

The first step when approaching a new layer is to remove the names of the current managers from consideration. They should be moved to a "parking lot" for later consideration. We want Business Head 1 to make decisions about managerial positions without being influenced by the current incumbents.

The second step is to compare the span of control of the managers on layer 3 with the target for this company, as shown in the table below. The target is based on data about the industry, geographic footprint, and complexity of operations. For our hypothetical company, the target is eight. This is an average for the entire company, and does not necessarily apply to each manager: some managers may have higher spans than eight, some lower, but on average we expect the company to have a span of control of eight, i.e., eight direct reports for each manager.

Group	Span	Target	Delta	Issue?
Research	7	8	-1	
Engineering	8	8	0	
Marketing	3	8	-5	Yes
Corporate Sales	2	8	-6	Yes
Retail Sales	2	8	-6	Yes
Procurement	6	8	-2	Maybe
Operations	9	8	1	
Distribution	7	8	-1	
Service	8	8	0	

At first glance, the Research, Engineering, Operations, Distribution and Service managers look fine from a span of control perspective. The Procurement manager is a borderline case. The Marketing and the two Sales managers clearly have issues that need to be addressed. We will review all of the managers, in order of their delta from the target span. Why are there two Sales managers, both with very low spans of control? It seems intuitively obvious that these two groups should be merged together and managed by one person. Situations similar to this arise frequently for logical reasons, such as the following:

- A Sales management role was created to accommodate a valuable or loyal manager who has no other position.

- The two Sales groups may have been much larger at one time and required two managers, but when the groups were downsized the managers were not.

- Possibly one manager will be replacing the other in time, and this structure allows the company to test the new manager before he/she takes over.

- The two managers may do a lot of sales themselves and don't have time to manage more staff members.

This twin-manager structure may be appropriate, based on the specific circumstances. However, a situation with a span of control significantly below the target span needs to be examined carefully through a role redesign process to determine if it is a case of 'over-management' (i.e., too many managers).

The role redesign process may vary for different firms. However, there is a basic set of principles to be followed in any redesign process. The first principle of redesign has already been applied: separate the role from the individual. If the second Sales manager position was created merely to accommodate an employee without a position in the firm, then it will become apparent when the individual's name is removed from the position.

The second principle is to separate the past from the present. While it may be informative to know why we have reached this particular twin-manager structure, it should not cloud our judgment regarding what is the appropriate structure for the present and the future.

The third principle is that the responsibilities of the manager should be specified explicitly. Usually these duties are described in the manager's job description. The fourth principle is a corollary of the third: managers should not have individual contributor activities as part of their formal job description. Periodically all of us have to do things to help a customer or our teams that are not part of our job description, which is fine and normal, but it shouldn't regularly consume a significant amount of a manager's time. If a manager is expected to regularly handle such tasks, then it should be built into his or her position description, or, better yet, it should be reassigned to his or her subordinates. Let's make this tangible by looking at our case study.

The two Sales managers' job descriptions explicitly state that their roles are to manage their sales forces: hiring, training, setting goals, reviewing progress, and evaluating and rewarding performance. However, in addition, the managers periodically get involved in specific transactions to help 'close the deal'. Given their effectiveness, the managers spend so much time on transactions that they don't have time to fulfill their specified managerial duties. This results in two super salespeople, but their teams languish because they are not being trained, they are not receiving feedback, they are not being forced to fail or succeed, and, when they leave the company, they are not being replaced – all because the two managers are serving as sales people and not as sales managers. In this case it is important to exclude sales activities from the managers' role descriptions. In the redesign of their roles we would reiterate that they are to build and run a sales force and not to contribute to the daily sales process.

Business Head 1 has to determine whether one manager can manage the Corporate and Retail markets, if the manager is no longer involved in transactions. In this case, he recognizes that the two sales managers were getting rewarded for their roles in closing transactions, instead of the overall results of their teams. He reviews the formal duties of a Sales manager and decides that the Retail and Corporate Sales should report to a single manager. When the two groups are merged, the Sales manager has a span of control of 4.

Business Head 1 has made progress in span of control optimization of the Sales group, and he may have more work to do. However, now the Marketing group has become a bigger issue, so he turns his attention there. This particular company has a Corporate Marketing group that reports to the Chief Operating Officer and was designed to provide centralized marketing support for all businesses. So why does Business Head 1 have a small Marketing team? Because his predecessor felt that the central Corporate Marketing group was not providing everything the business needed, and so he created his own Marketing team, which is a violation of our fifth principle.

The fifth principle is to forbid shadow organizations. Or, in other words, do not allow a manager to do work that is the responsibility of another group. If a service group is not satisfying the needs of the company, then fix the service group.

Do not create fixes all over the firm: not only is this inefficient, but it adds new problems, such as coordination between the Marketing groups, mandate confusion, and other complexities.

This particular Marketing group is serving two functions: providing some of the support that should come from Corporate Marketing and, second, placing advertisements, which is not within Corporate Marketing's mandate. This advertising activity is linked closely to the Sales group. To apply the fifth principle, Business Head 1 moves the advertising activity under the Sales manager, creates a stronger service level agreement with the Corporate Marketing group, and eliminates the Marketing manager reporting to him. His redesigned group is shown below.

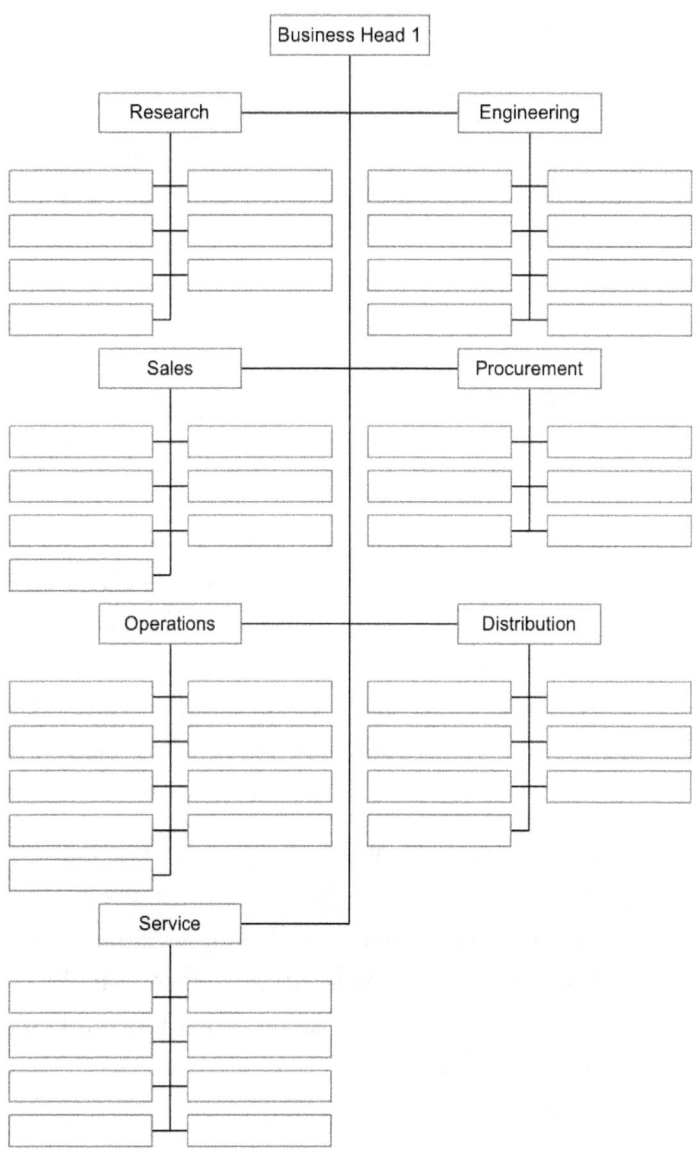

Now that Business Head 1 has settled on a group structure, the next step is to put manager names back onto the organization chart. The goal is to put the best manager into each open position. The managers of Research, Engineering, Procurement, Operations, Distribution and Service will likely return as the leaders of their groups. However, three names will remain in the "parking lot", that of the two Sales managers and the Marketing Head, but there is only one position available, the Sales position. Business Head 1 has to choose the best candidate, and the other two will remain in the parking lot, available for open positions in other parts of the firm, or for positions outside of the firm. Business Head 1 may have more work to do, but for the present time the work on his organization's structure is sufficient. The Reengineering team should look at the efforts by other groups and see if there are any potential synergies with this group.

While Business Head 1 is busy redesigning his group, the other managers on layer 2 are going through a similar exercise. Business Head 2 has a similarly structured group. However, she has encountered a different issue. The diagram below shows her organization, after the names of direct reports have been removed.

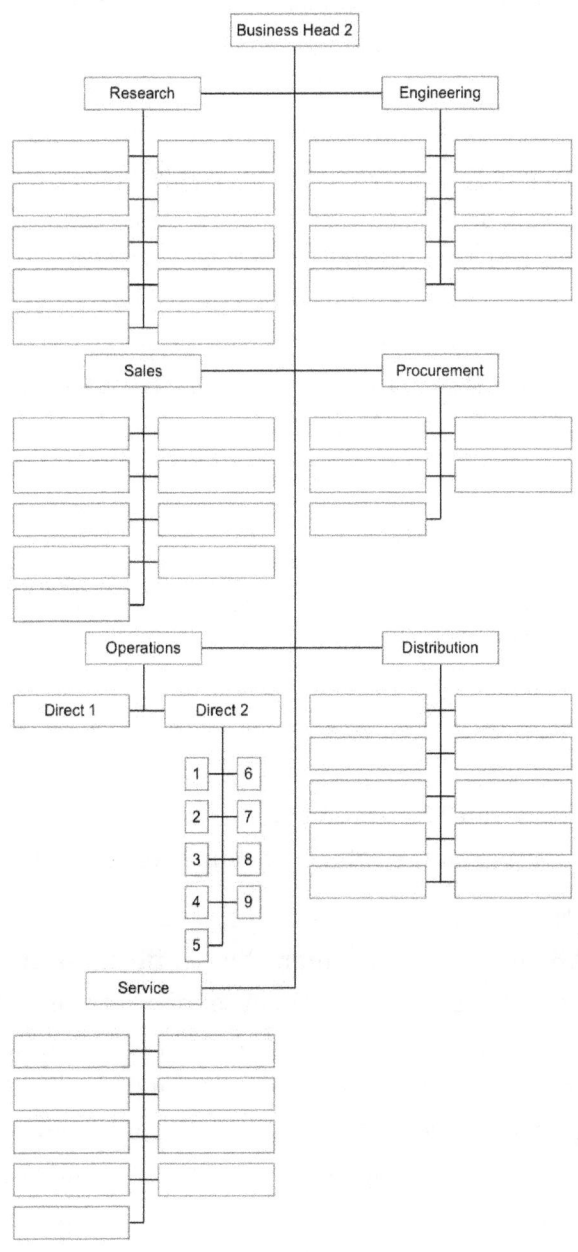

We have shown layers 2 through 4; for Operations we have also shown layer 5. Focusing on Operations, we can see that there are two direct reports on layer 4. However, one of those direct reports has nine direct reports on layer 5 (the small boxes). This structure may be the result of several different causes. In this case, Direct 2 has risen up through the ranks and is effectively managing Operations. Direct 2 could move up to layer 3, but there is nowhere in the organization for the current Operations manager to go. The Operations manager on layer 3 is truly a redundant employee. This leads to our sixth principle: a low-span manager with a high-span direct report is likely redundant. In this case, Direct 2 and the Operations manager roles are combined, which reduces a management layer. It is likely that when Business Head 2 moves the names from the parking lot back into her group chart that the former Operations manager will no longer be considered the best choice for this role.

Now that managers on layer 2 have redesigned layer 3, and chosen the managers to fill those positions, it is now time for them to instruct those managers to redesign layer 4. At this point we can see another advantage of starting the redesign process with the CEO and cascading down the layers of the organization; if the CEO and the

CEO's direct reports have participated in the process, then they will be committed to the process and will convey that commitment to managers below them and throughout the organization.

Hurdles

You will encounter resistance while redesigning your firm's management structure. Some of this resistance will be due to a lack of understanding by managers, and some will be due to an unwillingness to change; let's address these two cases sequentially. We'll begin with a deeper discussion about managers, so that we fully understand why redesign is important and necessary, and so that we can explain our motivation in detail to employees.

It is likely that anyone reading this text is a manager. How did you become manager? Did you go to management school, and then accept a position as a manager in a company? Probably not. The typical career path for a manager is to begin as an apprentice in some area of the company and work for many years to become a knowledgeable, competent professional in that area.

For example, a young person graduates from college with a degree in accounting, works for a company many years in the tax accounting department, and eventually, maybe 10, 15, or 20 years later, becomes one of the most competent and senior members of the department. Let's refer to him as Senior Accountant. When the current manager of that department retires, Senior

Accountant is tapped on the shoulder to be the new manager of that department. This is a typical path to a manager position.

Now that our Senior Accountant has management responsibilities, the company will likely encourage him to have manager training. Over the next few years, he takes courses in public speaking, organizational dynamics, leadership, and some annual Personnel Department training on how to run performance reviews. He still spends much of his time doing tax accounting, but he also spends some of his time doing his manager work: he has a weekly staff meeting, assigns work to his staff, reviews their work, goes to his manager's staff meeting and gives updates, occasionally deals with an employee issue, periodically hires a new person, and does performance reviews annually. Senior Accountant may not believe that he will ever be promoted to his manager's position because he doesn't have the breadth of knowledge and experience to manage areas outside of tax accounting.

Recently our Senior Accountant has encountered an issue with one of his best employees, a junior accountant who we will refer to as Junior. He started in the tax department several years after Senior, but he is a quick study, ambitious, successfully completes every assignment, and now seems bored in his role. Recently Junior has been hinting that he has learned everything he can in Senior's group and he is thinking about moving out of the group to a position that will add to his portfolio of skills. After several discussions, Senior learns that Junior would like to get experience as a manager, something he has not yet had the opportunity to do. This is problematic for Senior because he is the only manager in his group, and Junior can't have his job because he has nowhere else to go in the organization. He decides to create a new management position for Junior; half of his group will report to Junior, who will still report to him. This seems like a perfectly obvious way to handle this situation. Junior gets his management experience; Senior keeps Junior in the group.

Junior has not yet had any management training, but he has just learned his first big (and incorrect) lesson on management from Senior – if you have an unhappy employee, divide the group and create a new management position for that employee. It seems so smart, it didn't cost Senior a cent; he just rearranged lines in his organization chart. Senior's span of control was halved and a new management layer was created. There is a cost to the company, but it is difficult for Senior and Junior to see it in isolation. It is a cost that adds up across the organization.

A manager, according to the dictionary, is a person who controls and manipulates resources and expenditures. Are Senior and Junior managers? Not by this definition. Instead, they are tax accounts with some supervisory duties. They have spent their careers being tax accounting experts, their tax accounting expertise has been responsible for their promotions, and tax accounting remains their central interest and their source of power in the organization.

Senior's and Junior's promotions and manager training experiences are typical, and occur every day all over the world. Unfortunately companies typically do not set strict rules about organizational structure and don't have groups responsible for keeping their management structures lean. Instead, manager promotions blossom throughout an organization until the company has a cost problem, then layers of middle management are eliminated, the managers are terminated, and a restructuring charge destroys several years of earnings. If you closely follow some large companies over many years, you can watch the periodic cycle of building managerial bloat, followed by an army of consultants descending on the company, heavy cost cutting and layoffs, and then a large restructuring charge. Through an example we have portrayed the current situation in many companies. Now we will describe a preferred scenario.

Senior follows the same path as before, working his way up through the ranks of the tax accounting group and is then promoted. Senior never thought much about a manager role until now; he was always focused on his tax accounting work. Senior takes some time to reflect on the consequences of his promotion. He looks around at the different managers in the company, he observes them in company meetings, he looks at their organizations in the company directory, and he tries to understand their ascent through the ranks of the firm.

The senior managers seem alike in many respects: they're great communicators, they know how to inspire the troops, they manage many people, and they seem knowledgeable about many different subjects, such as research, engineering, marketing, finance, operations, distribution and personnel issues. Senior makes a startling observation: the CEO and the senior managers don't seem to do any "real work" -- they only manage other people. They control and manipulate resources and expenditures.

Senior is inspired to be a senior leader of the company someday, maybe even CEO. In his new role as manager he delegates his old duties to others in his group, and spends his time learning how to make his team perform at its highest level possible. As his management skills improve, he welcomes any opportunity to increase his span of control and his influence in the organization. When he has the opportunity, he spends time learning about other areas in the company and building his network. He realizes that spending half his day on the intricacies of tax accounting is not going to get him to the next level in the company. He is working for an opportunity on the next layer of the organization and he is trying to demonstrate that he has the broad knowledge and the management skills to handle it. Other executives notice Senior's rapid rise in the firm and they begin mimicking his attitude and approach. Over time these ambitious executives begin consolidating the low-span manager positions, which leads to a high-span, low-layer firm.

Through our example we have illustrated a common organizational state and what could be its future state. Migrating from one state to the other may be difficult because you will likely have to change the culture of the firm regarding the role of managers. Starting at the top of the firm, managers on each layer should be responsible for educating the layer below them. On every management layer you will likely encounter the same questions and objections about organization redesign. Below we have listed the objections we have encountered and our replies:

"Our managers are player-coaches" – this is an excuse for having many low-span managers. In addition to doing 'real work' (player), they also manage staff (coach). This is a poor excuse; player-coaches don't have enough time to be great managers. There is a reason why sports teams have dedicated coaches and are not coached by players. No person can optimize their performance and the team's simultaneously.

"Giving a high-performer a few people to manage gives them a feeling of advancement" – forget it, there are better ways of rewarding and advancing high-performers without creating a bigger problem for the organization. If Junior is a high performer and the firm believes he has the potential to be a great manager, then it should train him to be a manager and then give him a real management assignment. Giving him a small group, while expecting him to continue to be a high-performing individual contributor, does not teach him to be a real manager and does not help the firm.

"Our managers like to stay in the game" – managers need to keep abreast of developments in their field, and constantly expand their scope as well. But they should not be doing their subordinates' work. In the case of our fictitious employee Senior, he needs to keep abreast of changing tax laws, but he shouldn't be filing tax returns. Many high-performing employees are given management roles, but they don't enjoy or excel at managing – these employees should be given the opportunity to return to their individual contributor roles.

"We can't afford to not have our managers do real work" – this is the surest sign that the firm has too many managers. The firm should pare the management staff until the managers have no time to act as individual contributors.

"Corporate doesn't give us what we need" – that may be true, but replicating staff functions through small shadow organizations in the businesses creates more work, communication headaches, and destroys economies of scale. A better approach is to require Corporate support functions to serve the firm adequately.

Some managers will not embrace the new culture. They will be threatened by it, they will dismiss redesign as a fad, and they will try to thwart your efforts. Typically in any redesign effort there will be managers who no longer have roles within the company, and the uncooperative managers remaining in the parking lot are likely to be the managers who need to leave your company.

Implementation

The complexity of an organization redesign project depends on the degree of redesign contemplated. However, all projects have the same basic phases:

- *Diagnostic Phase* – gather data, compute spans and layers, compare with industry benchmarks, and estimate the cost savings opportunity.

- *Objectives Phase* – based on the diagnostic results, decide the goals of the project (e.g., 20% reduction in management), the team, and the time frame.

- *Design Phase* – determine if the objectives can be met by optimizing the current operating model, or if the organization's structure needs to be completely redesigned.

- *Structure and Staff Phase* – starting at the top of the organization, examine each layer's mandate, processes, and staff. Redesign each layer for increased spans of control; choose managers for redesigned positions.

- *Monitor Phase* – after completing the project, continue to monitor the organization to ensure that the management bloat does not creep back in.

The implementation of an organization redesign program is accomplished through a typical project management process. If you decide to launch a full-time organization redesign project, then we would expect that your project would have a sponsor, an executive steering committee, a working group, potentially external consultants, representatives from Human Resources supplying employee data, representatives from Finance providing financial data, representatives from Legal providing support for potential staff reductions, a project calendar, a schedule of briefings, a Gantt chart showing project dependencies, a communication plan for employees, and a set of guidelines for managers to help guide them with the redesign process and briefings for their managers. If the items in the list are not familiar to you, then you will likely need to bring in project management support. Let's now dig a little deeper into each phase.

Diagnostic Phase

This phase provides an assessment of your firm's spans and layers versus industry benchmarks. It also estimates the approximate annual personnel expense savings if you were to optimize the management structure.

<u>Benchmarking</u> is a fancy word for comparing your firm's average span of control and number of organizational layers to those of your competitors or similar types of firms. For example, if your 5,000 person firm has an average span of control of 3 and 9 layers of management (a steep and narrow pyramid), and your competitors have a span of 20 and 4 layers of management (a short and broad pyramid), you know that your firm probably has a problem.

Benchmarking is not always as simple as our example above. First, you need a way to calculate your firm's spans of control and layers of management. If you have a small firm, then you can do it with a pencil and paper. However, the calculation becomes much more difficult for medium and large organizations. In these cases software is required to do the work. A second complication is that your competitive benchmarks (the spans and layers of your competitors) are probably not readily available.

Spans and layers benchmarks for your company is probably one area where external consultants can be helpful to you. Consulting firms that do reengineering for a living see many companies and collect benchmarks for different industries. For example, if your firm's business is investment banking, consultants know roughly what are the spans and layers benchmarks for a professional services firm. Those benchmarks will be very different from, say, a call center.

Comparing your company's average spans of control and total number of layers with industry benchmarks is a good first step, but there is an equally important second step: comparing subsets of the company to benchmarks as well.

A company whose firm-wide average span of control is within industry norms may have problems that are masked by averaging. For example, the European arm of the firm might have an average span of control of 20, while the US is 10, and Asian is 5. The company might show a respectable total firm average of 12, which is masking issues in Asia. Similarly, a diagnostic analysis should look at the organizations for different businesses and support groups in the firm. Because different parts of the firm have different functions, they may require different benchmarks.

Cost savings estimates are the first thought that comes to mind when senior leaders realize that they have too many managers and organization optimization is required. Similarly, leaders will probably want to know the cost of terminating unnecessary managers. These exact costs will not be known until the actual individuals who need to leave the firm have been identified. However, there is an approximate method for estimating these savings.

Each layer of the organization (CEO is on layer 1, his/her direct reports on layer 2, etc) has a range of compensations. The company's human resources department should be able to provide an average total compensation amount for each layer of the organization. By knowing how many managers we expect to remove from each layer, we can compute the total annual savings produced by removing unnecessary managers.

The leadership team can use this savings estimate to decide whether an organization optimization project, and the associated disruption to the firm, is warranted by the estimated savings.

Objectives Phase

Based on the diagnostic results, in this phase the team decides the goals of the project, the team, and the time frame.

Goals: typically an industry benchmark average span of control is chosen as the project goal. If the goal is too aggressive, it may be tempered to ensure the project does not overly disrupt the firm's operations.

Team: the CEO and senior manager support are essential for success. Equally important for success is competent project management. The managers in the organization need to be deeply committed and involved in the redesign process, but they should not run the process.

There are several groups that are candidates for managing the redesign process:

- Reengineering Team – some organizations have internal reengineering teams whose mandate is to shape the organization and make it more efficient. These groups have strong project management skills, they are familiar with the firm, and their permanence allows them to manage the process over a long period of time. For all of these reasons this type of group is a natural candidate to run a redesign process. There are two potential downsides of this type of group. First, if the group is politically weak or there is sensitivity about this group being associated with layoffs, it may not be a wise choice. Second, if the group has never been through this before, and they need to do a full-fledged redesign of the entire company, then they may wish to hire a consulting firm specializing in redesign processes, at least for the first effort. The greatest benefit of having an internal reengineering group involved is it can continue to monitor the organization as part of their mandate, so that the organization does not slowly return to a bloated state over time.

- An internal task force, comprised of strategy and/or finance employees, is another possibility. In this case we need to make sure that the task force has the appropriate project management skills or they will likely not be successful. This team also has the advantage that it is familiar with the company. However, the downside is that this task force may not be familiar with organization redesign and it is transient – once the project is completed they will not likely remain involved in tracking the company. If you choose this option, then folks from Human Resources should be involved and they should have the mandate to continue monitoring the organization after the redesign project is completed.

- A third common approach is have the Human Resources department run the process with the strong support of consultants.

- Many consultants are well versed in organization redesign and project management. Whether you choose to use consultants may depend on how big and visible is the project and your team's skill level. If you do use consultants, it is critically important that you involve company staff who will be able to monitor the company after the consultants have left the premises.

Timeframe: the timeframe of a redesign process is highly dependent on the situation, the size of the company, the degree of redesign required, the company's geographic dispersion, and the schedules of senior management. A timeframe that is too short will lead to a hasty and ill-conceived organization; a timeframe that is too long will be unduly disruptive to the organization. For a typical mid-sized company, the timeframe would be as follows:

- Diagnostic Phase – one week is sufficient, if you have the appropriate data available.

- Objectives Phase – two weeks, provided you have access to senior management and the company has a Reengineering Team (or similar) available immediately.

- Design Phase – this depends on if you are optimizing the current model (a few weeks) or redesigning the organization's operating model (a few months).

- Structure and Staff Phase – two to three weeks for each layer. During the first week the managers have to be educated about the process, inform the staff of the work, and review their organization versus a target. In the second week the managers will need to review and edit their managers' job specifications, redesign their organization, and choose their managers. In some cases this will take longer than one week. Finally, in the third week, the managers will communicate the results back to their managers and prepare them for their work on their organizations.

- Monitor Phase – tracking reports should be published monthly during the redesign process and quarterly afterwards.

Design Phase

After the objectives, the timeframe, and the team have been decided, it is up to that team to decide what the new organizational design will be when the project is completed.

<u>Partial redesign</u> is adequate if there are pockets of the company that need to be optimized, some managers removed, but overall the structure of the organization is fine.

<u>Complete redesign</u> is required if there is no way to tweak the current model to meet the objectives. For example, a company that has a small organization in each state may determine that they need to streamline their organization to be regional, that is, an organization in four regions of the country: north, south, east, and west.

Similarly, they may decide that some product lines or services have too small a revenue contribution to warrant the level of management in place.

The design team cannot do the person-by-person organizational redesign of each group: that is up to the group leader and the reengineering team. However, the design team should decide which parts of the company need to be redesigned and optimized.

Structure and Staff Phase

Once we know which parts of the organization need to be addressed, and any design requirements for the organization, the structure and staffing phase is to work through the organization, starting at the top of the organization, examining each layer's mandate, processes, and staff sequentially. Redesign each layer for increased spans of control and eliminate unnecessary layers; choose managers for redesigned positions. Instruct those managers on the redesign process and charge them with redesigning their managers on the next layer. This process was discussed in the *Approach* chapter.

Monitor Phase

This starts with monitoring progress throughout the process and then afterwards quarterly to ensure that management bloat does not creep back in. Just like a firm periodically audits itself, periodically reviews its financial performance, and reviews the performance of its employees, it should periodically monitor its spans and layers to determine if it continues to be lean and structured optimally. The results of monitoring should be included in the management team's regular reporting.

Conclusion

Without disciplined efforts to stay fit, firms often grow to be bloated, bureaucratic and inefficient. Reducing layers of management and increasing manager spans of control is a time-tested method for improving a firm's fitness.

To become fit, an organization conducts a spans and layers project, which consists of the following phases: diagnosis, objectives, design, structuring, and staffing. Afterwards, it should periodically monitor its spans and layers to remain lean and structured optimally.

Organizations that successfully flatten and widen their management hierarchies don't just save money; they also improve decision making, enhance accountability, faster and more reliable communication, are more efficient, and their employees are happier.

Steffen Parratt has 30 years of experience serving a wide range of companies, from small startups to large global enterprises. He has a bachelor's and master's degree in mechanical and electrical engineering, respectively, from the University of Rochester, a master's and PhD in engineering from Cornell University, and an MBA from the Wharton School of the University of Pennsylvania.